HONEY

THE GOODNESS OF
HONEY

40 SWEET AND
SAVOURY RECIPES

EDITED BY **HANNAH COUGHLIN**
KYLE BOOKS

CONTENTS

6.
INTRODUCTION

14.
BREAKFAST

28.
LIGHT BITES
& SIDES

48.
MAINS

70.
SWEETS
& DRINKS

92.
INDEX

GOLDEN GOODNESS

The sweet nectar of honey has long been described as the food of the gods, and in many cultures it is believed to represent good health and prospects. Worldwide, it is a symbol of optimism and purity, and it has been consumed by humans for thousands of years. Hippocrates believed in honey as the great golden healer, while Pythagoras insisted it was in supply at his school of philosophy. The oldest evidence of honey being collected by humans dates to prehistoric times, in paintings found in caves near Valencia, Spain. They are thought to have originated in the Stone Age, some 15,000 years ago.

Honey is unique in that it comes only from honey bees – no scientist or company has been able to develop a machine or discover the means to manufacture it artificially. The raw material, nectar, is gathered laboriously from thousands of flowers before worker bees in hives turn it in to the golden deliciousness that is honey.

It is best to use raw, unprocessed honey. Honey is often filtered, or even ultra-filtered, which means it has been treated with heat. While this ensures that the honey stays liquid in the jar and keeps it an attractive colour, the process also removes the enzymes, vitamins, antioxidants and antibacterial benefits – all the nutritional properties that make honey so special. Honey that is crammed to bursting with pollen has a cloudier appearance – this is the best raw honey.

NATURE'S SWEETNESS

The natural sweetness of honey means it's a popular substitute for processed sugar, offering an alternative way to indulge your sweet tooth without the harmful properties of sugar.

Weight for weight, honey is sweeter than sugar, so less honey is needed than if you were using conventional sugar alone. If you're substituting runny honey for sugar in a baking recipe, you'll need to add less liquid to avoid the mixture becoming a soggy mess. Honey is also a preservative, so anything baked with honey should stay fresh for longer than alternatives, if stored in an airtight container, and extend the shelf life of your cakes or biscuits.

Although it makes a fantastic sweetener in baked goods, it's also a great way to add a sweet touch to savoury dishes. Honey will give a gorgeous dark colour to roast meats and a wonderful crispness to the browned skin, as well as a caramelised sweetness to roast vegetables.

How to store

Do not store jars of honey in the fridge. Honey is best kept at room temperature, which will prevent the rapid crystallisation that naturally develops in honey over time. To return crystallised honey to its liquid form, simply sit the jar in a bowl of hot water for about 15 minutes. Alternatively, you can remove the lid and put the jar in the microwave for 15 seconds. Repeat this process if necessary.

Honey won't go off because it is acidic, high in sugar, and antibacterial, all of which will kill off germs.

A great tip when spooning out honey is to coat the spoon in the thinnest layer of mild olive oil (or other flavourless oil) – the honey will simply slide off the spoon.

TYPES OF HONEY

There are a wide variety of honeys available, each characterised by local blossoms. Different blends of wild flora will impact on the flavour and appearance of each type. Lighter honeys have a more fragrant and delicate flavour, while darker honeys are stronger and richer. In general, darker honey has a higher bioflavonoid content and greater antibacterial benefits. It also tends to be less processed and so have a higher mineral content. Common types of honey include:

Acacia
Light-coloured, clear honey that is delicately flavoured. It will stay liquid almost indefinitely.

Balsam
A refreshing honey with a light colour and taste, often collected by bees at the water's edge.

Borage
A less common variety worth looking out for. Light-coloured with a richer taste than acacia, it was a favourite of the Romans.

Hawthorn
A mature and hearty flavour, celebrated in folklore for relieving hypertension and heart palpitations.

Heather
A strong honey, with an almost jelly-like consistency, that reflects the colour of heather. It is packed with minerals and also has high antibacterial properties.

Hedgerow
The variation in plants means hedgerow honey can differ dramatically depending on where and when it is made, but it is always rich and deep.

Lavender
Some find this excessively perfumed, but its rich, dark and aromatic qualities make it irresistible to others.

Oilseed Rape
A soft set honey with a thicker consistency to avoid crystallisation. It's less likely to create a sticky mess than liquid honey.

Orange Blossom
Identifiable by its rich amber colour and tangy taste, this honey will remain runny for some time.

Sweet Chestnut
Dark flavoured with a slightly burnt taste, and full of antibacterial content.

Tupelo
From the swamplands of Northwest Florida, this light honey has a deep mellow taste and is thinner than more common honeys.

Wildflower
A more difficult honey to source, as wildflower meadows are dying out. The taste varies according to the local flowers.

Super Honey

Some honeys can be classed as 'super honey' as they are exceptionally high in antibacterial content. These extra health-giving properties are a result of the bees visiting superior plants during production. In general, the darker the honey, the greater its antibacterial and antifungal properties and its mineral and vitamin content. Manuka is the best-know super honey, and comes from a family of tea tree plants in New Zealand, which produce tea tree oils.

MEDICAL MARVEL

Honey has been used to treat all kinds of ailments for thousands of years and its medicinal use can be traced back to Ancient Roman, Greek and Chinese cultures. But although honey is often the first thing many of us reach for when we are coming down with a sore throat or scratchy cough – soothing honey eases pain and restores energy – many people know very little about it's other healing properties.

◆ Honey is antibacterial and antifungal and can be used to treat infected wounds. Research in New Zealand has indicated that it may heal and restore anything from wounds and ulcers to serious burns.

◆ Honey has a gentle laxative effect and supports friendly gut bacteria, aiding digestion throughout the day.

◆ It has no side effects due to its pure nature. The World Health Organisation recommends honey as a cough and cold remedy, even for acute respiratory infections in children.

◆ Honey boosts the immune system and has an antibacterial effect both internally and externally, helping the body to heal.

◆ A spoonful of unprocessed honey before bed can support your brain function. Brain activity doesn't stop when you sleep, and the fructose in honey is stored as energy in the liver, providing a continuous energy supply overnight.

◆ The list of ailments that honey is said to help alleviate is long (though not all the claims for it have been scientifically proven). These include: wounds, burns, gastric ulcers, IBS, thrush, constipation, water retention, conjunctivitis, cataracts, hay fever, colds, coughs, sore throats, night cramps, insomnia, bed-wetting, bed sores, rheumatism, blood pressure, infertility, baldness, lice and nits and memory loss. It is also said to help ensure a healthy heart and aid weight loss.

Honey vs. Sugar

Honey contains more calories weight for weight than sugar, but you'll need to use less of it. It is also much more valuable health wise, especially if it is natural, unprocessed honey. Honey is made up of two types of sugar in almost equal parts: glucose and fructose. The body absorbs glucose quickly, giving an instant energy hit within seconds, but without the addition of fructose, this energy is short lived. Once the amount of glucose exceeds that needed by the body, it is transformed into fat, unless fructose is present. In which case, it is converted into a food reserve in the liver, where it is stored for when the body or brain next require it.

Beauty

Honey is also a fantastic ingredient in natural beauty solutions, and can be used for many homemade remedies such as a milk and honey bath soak, a hair shine rinse, face masks and even as a moisturiser.

Preserving

Honey and preserving have always gone hand in hand. In Ancient Egypt, important figures were even buried in a combination of honey, beeswax and propolis. Honey is still used today in the Middle East to preserve butter and cheese, which are smothered in honey to protect them during long hot journeys.

This is because honey is saturated with sugars that suck out water from bacteria and mould, making it impossible for any germs to survive. It dehydrates the living cells, disabling them and leaving them dormant. The acidity of honey also helps kill off the germs, while the thick and syrupy consistency ensures the acidity doesn't affect humans in the same way. In fact, honey often brings relief to those suffering from gastric reflux.

BAKED APPLE & CINNAMON OATMEAL

*VEGETARIAN *DAIRY-FREE *GLUTEN-FREE

This baked oatmeal makes a fantastic warming and hearty breakfast for chilly winter mornings. You could swap the dried fruit and nuts for any of your favourites.

Serves 4

150g gluten-free oats
500ml almond milk
4 eating apples, peeled, cored
  and chopped
4 teaspoons ground cinnamon
5 tablespoons raw honey
Juice of 1 lemon
50g raisins
A handful of flaked almonds
A handful of goji berries
2 tablespoons almond butter
1 teaspoon vanilla extract
A spoonful of coconut yogurt
  and a sprinkling of berries,
  to serve (optional)

1. Put the oats and the almond milk in a bowl and leave to soak.

2. Preheat the oven to 180°C/gas mark 4.

3. Put the apples, 1 teaspoon of the ground cinnamon, 1 tablespoon of the honey and all the lemon juice in a saucepan with a ladleful of water. Cook over a low heat until the apple has softened.

4. Mix the remaining cinnamon and honey together with all the other ingredients, except the yogurt and berries.

5. Once the apples have cooked, add them to the fruit and nut mixture then tip onto a baking tray and spread into an even layer. Bake for 15 minutes, then preheat the grill to medium-high, or switch the oven to the grill setting.

6. Grill for 5 minutes so the porridge gets a little crispy on top.

7. Serve with a spoonful of coconut yogurt and a sprinkling of berries.

BARRETTE CROCCANTI

*VEGETARIAN *DAIRY-FREE

Have you ever read the back of a cereal bar wrapper? You may be surprised to discover that, in many cases, they're not as good for you as you might have thought! 'Healthy' bars can contain as many calories and the same amount of fat as an ordinary chocolate bar or two packets of crisps. It pays to know what's in your food or, even better, make your own cereal bars so you can be sure they're good for you. This recipe is tasty, healthy and quick and easy to make.

Makes 14 bars

150g dried cranberries
100g dried apricots
60g shelled pistachio nuts
50g sunflower seeds
50g porridge oats
60g wholemeal flour
60ml orange juice
4 tablespoons runny honey

1. Preheat the oven to 190°C/ gas mark 5 and line a baking tray with greaseproof paper. Place the dried fruits in a food processor and blitz until roughly chopped.

2. Add the pistachio nuts, sunflower seeds, oats and flour. Pour in the orange juice with the honey and blitz again until roughly combined. Transfer the mixture to the prepared baking tray and spread out evenly with a knife until it is about 1cm thick.

3. Bake in the middle of the oven for 20 minutes until golden brown. Remove from the oven, leave to cool on the tray then slice into bars.

4. Keep in an airtight plastic container for up to a week.

Vary the nuts and fruit as much as you like and experiment with your favourite combinations.

FRUITY, NUTTY GRANOLA
*VEGETARIAN

This is a great recipe to use up store-cupboard items.
Halve the amount of sugar and coconut oil if you'd rather
make a muesli. You can use any honey for baking the
granola, but use your favourite raw honey for topping.

Makes approx. 1kg

200g mixed fruit, chopped if
   large (figs, apricots, dates)
100g dried cranberries, dried
   cherries or raisins (or a mix)
100g extra virgin coconut oil
2 teaspoons ground cinnamon
1 teaspoon vanilla extract
150ml honey
500g jumbo oats
150g nuts of your choice
   (almonds, walnuts,
   pistachios, pecans)
100g pumpkin seeds
100g sunflower seeds
75g desiccated coconut

To serve
Thick yogurt and/or milk
A drizzle of raw runny honey

1. Preheat the oven to 180°C/gas
mark 4 and line two large baking
trays with greaseproof paper.
Put all the fruit in a bowl and
just cover with boiling water. Set
aside for 10 minutes. Drain well.

2. Put the coconut oil, cinnamon
and vanilla extract in a small
saucepan and very gently melt
them together over a low heat.
Stir in the honey.

3. Put the oats, nuts, seeds and
coconut in a large bowl. Pour
over the oil and honey mixture
and stir well, making sure
everything is evenly coated.

4. Tip the mixture out onto the
prepared trays, spreading it out
evenly to the edges. Bake for 15
minutes, then remove from the
oven and stir in the drained and
dried fruit. (If you add it earlier,
it will harden too much in the
oven.) Return to the oven and
cook until evenly toasted and
golden, another 15–20 minutes.
Stir half way through.

5. Remove from the oven and
leave to cool completely, then
store in a airtight container.
Serve with thick yogurt and/or
milk, drizzled with honey – or just
munch on a handful as a snack!

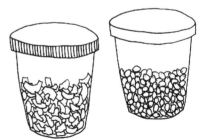

BERRY & HONEY TEFF PANCAKES

*VEGETARIAN *GLUTEN-FREE

Delicious nutty pancakes that are gluten free, too. Drizzle with a fragrant, golden, wildflower honey for a delicate finish, or a Greek variety if you like a deeper flavour.

Makes 16

100g teff flour
100g rice flour or oat flour
  (made by blitzing rolled oats
  to a fine powder in a
  powerful food-processor)
1 teaspoon baking powder
Large pinch of salt
¼ teaspoon mixed spice
1 free-range egg, beaten
1 teaspoon honey
200ml cow's, rice or oat milk
Butter or coconut oil, for
  cooking

To serve
Thick yogurt
A handful of berries of your
  choice (e.g. raspberries,
  blackberries or blueberries)
A drizzle of raw runny honey
A few hazelnuts, coarsely
  chopped

1. Sift the flours, baking powder, salt and mixed spice into a bowl. Make a well in the centre and add the egg, honey and milk. Whisk the mix to a smooth batter – it should be the consistency of thick cream, just dropping from the spoon.

2. In a large non-stick frying pan, heat a little butter or coconut oil. Drop in a tablespoon of the batter at a time, spacing each well apart. Cook for 1–2 minutes until bubbles appear and the underside is golden. Flip over and cook for a further 1–2 minutes, until golden.

3. Serve with dollops of yogurt, a scattering of berries and chopped hazelnuts and a drizzle of your favourite raw honey.

PEACH & RASPBERRY COMPOTE

*VEGETARIAN *DAIRY-FREE *GLUTEN-FREE

If you use the ripest and juiciest fruit possible the flavours will really sing, and you'll also need less honey to sweeten it. Perfect paired with ice cream or frozen yogurt.

Makes 1 x 500g jar

6 large very ripe peaches
6 tablespoons orange flower honey
½ teaspoon vanilla paste
200g raspberries

1. Cut the peaches in half, remove the stones and peel with a small knife. (The skin should come away easily if they are nice and ripe.) Cut into eighths and put into a pan with the honey and vanilla.

2. Cook the peaches very gently for 5–6 minutes, or until they are beginning to soften and break down. They should be very juicy, but if they are catching, add a couple of tablespoons of water.

3. Add the raspberries and cook another minute. Taste for a good balance of flavours and add more honey if necessary.

4. Cool, then tip into a sterilised jar (see below). The compote will keep for 2 weeks in the fridge.

To sterilise glass containers, wash them in hot, soapy water, rinse well, then dry with a clean cloth. Place in an oven, without the lids, 120°C/gas mark ½ for 10 minutes until dry. If using kilner jars, remove the rubber seals and boil them to avoid damage in the oven.

PLUM & BLACKBERRY COMPOTE

Mildly spiced and wonderfully warming on a cold autumnal morning. Add a dollop to porridge or yogurt.

Makes 1 x 500g jar

8 ripe plums
3 tablespoons orange flower
  honey (or more depending
  on sweetness of the plums)
1 star anise
½ cinnamon stick
300g blackberries

1. Wash the plums and cut them in half, then remove the stones and cut each half into quarters. Place in a pan with the honey, star anise, cinnamon and 100ml water. Cook over a medium heat until the plums begin to soften and break down a little, about 5 minutes, then add the blackberries and cook for a further 1–2 minutes. The blackberries should soften but still hold their shape.

2. Cool and then taste, adding a little more honey if necessary. Spoon into a sterilised jar and keep for up to 2 weeks in the fridge. Enjoy warm or chilled.

BAKED ENERGY
BARS *VEGETARIAN

Raw honey is a great energy and essential bioactive boost, and is far better for you than sugar-packed cereals. Keep it natural and serve with fresh fruit to add to the already high bioflavonoid content of the honey.

Serves 2

350ml honey
3 tablespoons butter
175g caster sugar
600g plain flour
1 teaspoon baking powder
½ teaspoon bicarbonate of
   soda
¼ teaspoon ground ginger
2 teaspoons ground cinnamon
Pinch of ground cloves
55g candied cherries, chopped
55g candied orange peel
40g chopped almonds

1. Preheat the oven to 180°C/ gas mark 4. Melt the honey, butter and sugar together in a large saucepan.

2. In a separate bowl combine half the flour, the baking powder, bicarbonate of soda and spices. Mix well.

3. Add the melted butter mixture to the dry ingredients and stir well. Stir in the candied fruits and almonds with the remaining flour. The mixture should be very sticky; to add a little more moisture, mix in 2-3 tablespoons of honey.

4. Spoon into two lined baking trays and bake in the oven for 30 minutes. Remove and cut into squares. Leave to cool – the squares will become soft and chewy. Store in an airtight container to keep as treats for weeks to come.

INSTANT
ENERGY DRINK

Honey can provide energy within seven minutes, according to research on athletes. It also provides a slow-burn effect that produces great stamina and endurance. The free fructose and glucose sugars in honey restore brain activity constantly, thus reducing or eliminating fatigue at times of our greatest physical and mental need. This is an easy way to harness these benefits during your morning routine.

Serves 4

2 litres boiled water
200g of unprocessed honey
3g salt
Juice of 1–2 lemons

1. Pour the water into a large saucepan. Add the honey and salt and simmer over a medium heat until both are dissolved. Then add the lemon juice and stir to combine.

2. Leave to cool then transfer to the fridge to chill for 2–3 hours before drinking.

LIGHT BITES & SIDES

HONEY BEETROOT & FETA *VEGETARIAN *GLUTEN-FREE

Fresh beetroot takes a long time to cook. However, in the chilled vegetable section of the supermarket, you can often find vacuum-packed cooked beetroot. It's a brilliant ingredient to use in quick recipes, as the long, boring bit of the cooking has been done for you.

Serves 4

3 x 250g packets of cooked beetroot
2 tablespoons extra virgin olive oil
2 tablespoons runny honey
A few sprigs of thyme
3 tablespoons balsamic vinegar
100g feta
Salt and freshly ground black pepper, to taste

1. Put a large frying pan over a high heat.

2. Remove the beetroot from the packet and quarter each one.

3. Add the oil to the pan then the beetroot. Fry for 2 minutes before stirring in the honey and thyme. Cook for a further 2 minutes to allow the honey to caramelise.

4. Pour in the vinegar and deglaze the pan by stirring continuously with a wooden spoon.

5. Allow everything to bubble for 1 minute then spoon out into a serving bowl.

6. Crumble over the feta, season to taste and serve.

DAIKON & CARROT
SALAD *VEGETARIAN *DAIRY-FREE *GLUTEN-FREE

Serves 4

1 daikon or Japanese white
  radish (about 400g),
  finely sliced into 5cm long
  matchsticks
1 teaspoon fine salt
4 tablespoons rice vinegar
2 carrots, finely sliced into
  5cm long matchsticks

For the dressing

2 teaspoons sesame oil
2 teaspoons clear honey,
  preferably raw
½ teaspoon grated fresh
  ginger
1 teaspoon toasted black
  sesame seeds

Daikon has numerous health benefits; it is high in fibre, low in fat and full of vitamin C, potassium and phosphorus. A mandoline makes quick work of the preparation. Serve with quickly seared rare tuna or mixed with a few pea shoots.

1. Put the daikon in a bowl and sprinkle generously with the salt and 1 tablespoon of the vinegar. Leave for 10 minutes, thoroughly squeeze, then transfer to a bowl of iced water for another 10 minutes. Drain and squeeze thoroughly again. This removes the bitter taste and keeps it crisp.

2. In a serving bowl, mix the daikon with the carrots (use your fingers to separate any clumps of squeezed daikon).

3. In a small jug, mix the dressing ingredients. Pour over the daikon and carrot mix and leave to stand for 30 minutes before serving.

CUCUMBER SALAD

Serves 6

4 Japanese cucumbers or
  2 large English cucumbers
  (about 600g)
1½ teaspoons sea salt flakes

For the dressing

3 teaspoons mild clear honey,
  preferably raw
2 tablespoons rice vinegar
2 teaspoons tamari
2 teaspoons toasted black and
  white sesame seeds

This is great served with salmon, mackerel or other oily fish as it cuts through the richness wonderfully. Traditional Japanese recipes typically cut the cucumber in fine ribbons or very thin slices, but thicker chunks add a lovely crunch.

1. Peel the cucumbers, cut them in half lengthways, deseed if using English cucumbers and then cut into diagonal 5mm slices. Sprinkle with the salt, toss together and leave for 30 minutes in a bowl lined with kitchen paper, for the cucumber to release some of its juice.

2. Meanwhile, mix the dressing ingredients together.

3. After 30 minutes, quickly rinse and pat the cucumber dry, then transfer to a bowl, pour over the dressing and toss together. Taste and add extra honey/stevia if you like. Leave in a cool place or refrigerate for 1 hour before serving.

FIG-LEAF
WRAPPED FETA
*VEGETARIAN *GLUTEN-FREE

Greek mountains are full of fragrant fig trees, but the leaves are rarely used. This combination of seasonal ingredients makes perfect sense – they are made for each other. If you don't have a barbecue, a regular oven will do!

Serves 4

4 large fresh fig leaves, washed and dried
2 x 200g packets of feta, cut in half
4 figs, torn into pieces
16 whole, skin-on almonds, roughly chopped
4 tablespoons runny honey

1. Preheat the barbecue or oven to 220°C/gas mark 7. Lay the fig leaves, vein-side up, on a work surface and place a piece of feta on top of each. Fold over the leaves to make a neat parcel. Place between two barbecue grills, or on a wire rack on top of a baking tray if cooking in the oven.

2. Place the parcels on the barbecue or in the oven and cook for 5–8 minutes until the feta has begun to soften when squeezed and the leaves are fragrant.

3. Remove the parcels from the oven, open them up and top the feta with the figs and almonds. Drizzle with honey and serve immediately in the leaves.

Use vine leaves if fig leaves are unavailable.

KNOCKOUT SALAD
DRESSINGS *VEGETARIAN *DAIRY-FREE

CHILLI BALSAMIC VINAIGRETTE

Delicious drizzled over beetroot, steamed or grilled asparagus, and raw or pan-fried courgette.

Serves 4–6

4 tablespoons olive oil
2 tablespoons balsamic vinegar
2 tablespoons lime or orange juice
1 tablespoon honey
1 teaspoon soy sauce
1 chilli, halved and deseeded

Place all the ingredients in a jam jar. Shake and store in the fridge for up to 1 week.

SUMMER HERB VINAIGRETTE

Lovely with summer courgettes cut into ribbons, radishes, crunchy lettuce leaves, green beans, and more.

Serves 4–6

A large handful of fresh, soft green herbs
   (e.g. basil, coriander, mint, tarragon),
   finely chopped
100ml olive oil
3 tablespoons cider or white wine vinegar
Zest of 1 lemon
1 teaspoon honey
Sea salt and black pepper

Place all the ingredients in a jam jar. Shake and store in the fridge for 1–2 days.

HONEY MUSTARD THYME

Gorgeous with a simple salad of grated carrots or crunchy leaves.

Serves 4–6

4 tablespoons olive oil
3 tablespoons grainy or Dijon mustard
2 tablespoons honey
½ garlic clove, finely minced
2 teaspoons fresh thyme leaves
Sea salt and black pepper

Place all the ingredients in a jam jar. Shake well to fully mix in the honey. Store in the fridge for up to 1 week.

SESAME GINGER LIME

Perfect on a salad of crunchy leaves with chunks of mango, freshly grated coconut, toasted cashews or macadamias and fresh coriander leaves. Or use it to dress warm carrots, beans or peas.

Serves 4–6

125ml sesame oil
4 tablespoons lime juice
1 tablespoon honey
1 tablespoon soy sauce
3cm piece of fresh ginger, peeled and
   finely chopped

Place all the ingredients in a jam jar. Shake and store in the fridge for up to 1 week.

FOOLPROOF ROOT VEGETABLES

*VEGETARIAN *GLUTEN-FREE

The root veg family are a tasty old bunch and for me, roasted root veg are a staple for many a winter dish and can help make or break a roast dinner. Blanching root vegetables first ensures they don't have that woody flavour that is sometimes evident otherwise.

Serves 6 as a side

600g carrots, halved
  lengthways
600g parsnips, halved
  lengthways
800g turnips, quartered
2 stalks of celery, cut into
  chunks
3 tablespoons clear honey
  (Spanish Blossom if
  possible)
2 tablespoons truffle oil
Leaves from 1 sprig of thyme
Leaves from 1 sprig of
  rosemary
2 garlic cloves, crushed
100g butter, cut into 10g
  cubes
Salt and freshly ground
  black pepper

1. Preheat the oven to 200°C/gas mark 6.

2. Bring a large pan of salted water to the boil. Add the carrots, parsnips and turnips and blanch them for 7 minutes. Drain and allow to cool.

3. Place the blanched veg and celery on a roasting tray, drizzle with honey and truffle oil and scatter over the herbs. Dot the cubes of butter over the veg. Season well and roast for 20 minutes, or until the veg starts to caramelise slightly.

TOMATO, HONEY & CHILLI SOUP

*VEGETARIAN *GLUTEN-FREE

This is a great comforting staple; whenever you're feeling
a little tender, this pick-me-up is exactly what's needed.
Serve it with croutons and semi-dried tomatoes, or a good
old classic ham and cheese sandwich to dip in.

Serves 4

2 tablespoons olive oil
50g butter
2 red onions, finely chopped
2 garlic cloves, crushed
1 stalk of celery, chopped
½ red chilli, deseeded and
   roughly chopped
2 x 400g cans chopped
   tomatoes
400ml vegetable stock
1 tablespoon dried oregano
1 tablespoon dried thyme
2 tablespoons clear honey
Salt and freshly ground black
   pepper

For the semi-dried tomatoes
6 cherry tomatoes, halved
20g dried oregano

For the croutons
4 slices day-old bread, cut
   into squares

1. In a medium saucepan, heat
the oil and butter. When hot,
add the onions, garlic, celery
and chilli and fry for about 10
minutes, or until softened.

2. Add the chopped tomatoes,
stock, dried herbs and seasoning
and allow to simmer for at least
30 minutes.

3. While the soup is bubbling
away, make the toppings for the
soup. Preheat the oven to 150°C/
gas mark 2. Place the tomatoes
on a baking tray, sprinkle with
the oregano and salt. Pop the
bread squares on a separate tray.
Transfer both trays to the oven
and bake for 40 minutes.

4. Add the honey to the soup,
then blend the soup with a stick
blender until smooth.

5. Remove the tomatoes and
bread from the oven and sprinkle
over the soup to serve.

HONEY, LIME & SOY KING PRAWNS

*DAIRY-FREE

The biggest, juiciest prawns are often found in the Far East, where there inspiration for this recipe comes from. It makes the perfect holiday food!

Serves 4

16 large raw king prawns, peeled and deveined
1 tablespoon dark soy sauce
2 tablespoons blossom honey
Zest and juice of 1 lime
2 teaspoons olive oil
100g (about 2) baby pak choi, sliced

1. Rinse the prawns and pat dry on kitchen paper. Pour the soy sauce into a small saucepan. Add the honey, lime zest and juice. Bring to the boil, then reduce the heat and simmer over a low heat for 4–5 minutes until reduced by half and syrupy. Remove from the heat and set aside.

2. Heat a large wok or non-stick frying pan over a high heat for 1 minute. Add the olive oil and heat for 30 seconds. Add the prawns and stir-fry over a high heat for 15 seconds. Add the soy sauce syrup and stir-fry for a further 15 seconds. Add the pak choi and stir-fry for 10–20 seconds until the leaves are just wilted (don't overcook the pak choi or its water content will make the sauce too runny). Serve immediately.

JASMINE TEA & HONEY CHICKEN SKEWERS

*DAIRY-FREE *GLUTEN-FREE

Jasmine tea is scented with the perfume of jasmine blossoms. Typically made with green tea as the base, it is probably the most famous scented tea in China. It goes particularly well with chicken, giving these skewers a subtle, sweet taste with a distinctive, smoky flavour.

Serves 4

200g skinless chicken breast fillets
Sesame seeds, to garnish
4 tablespoons vegetable oil

For the glaze
10g loose Jasmine tea leaves
50ml boiling water
4 tablespoons runny honey
2 teaspoons yellow mustard
1 teaspoon sugar
½ teaspoon salt
1cm piece of fresh ginger, peeled and grated
1 tablespoon sesame oil

1. Presoak 16 short wooden skewers for 30 minutes. Meanwhile, make the glaze. Place the tea leaves in a jug, pour over the boiling water and set aside to steep for 3 minutes. Strain into a small bowl, discarding the leaves, and stir in the honey, mustard, sugar, salt, ginger and sesame oil. Pour 5 tablespoons of glaze into a separate bowl and reserve for seving.

2. Slice the chicken breasts in half, and then lengthways into 3cm 'ribbons'. Halve each ribbon. Place the chicken in the honey and jasmine tea glaze. Cover the bowl with clingfilm and set aside in the fridge to marinate for 45 minutes.

3. Weave the marinated chicken strips onto the skewers.

4. In a dry pan over a medium heat, carefully toast the sesame seeds for 1 minute until they start to brown. Set aside.

5. Heat a frying pan with 2 tablespoons of oil over a medium heat and add the skewers. Cook the skewers on each side for 30 seconds. They will cook very quickly so use tongs to turn them frequently. Preheat a griddle pan over a high heat and add the remaining 2 tablespoons of oil. Transfer the skewers to the griddle pan and slightly sear them on each side for just 20 seconds, being careful not to burn them.

6. To serve, sprinkle the skewers with the toasted sesame seeds and accompany with the reserved glaze.

Using a griddle pan can easily burn this dish so an alternative is to grill the skewers for 5–8 minutes in the oven.

BALINESE CHICKEN
*DAIRY-FREE

A refreshing, mildly spiced chicken dish with Indonesian and Thai flavours. This would make an ideal canapé dish.

Serves 2

2 large organic, skinless
 chicken breasts

For the marinade
3 tablespoons crunchy peanut
 butter
2 tablespoons tamari
2 garlic cloves, grated
1 tablespoon runny honey
100ml coconut cream

For the dressing
1 garlic clove grated
3 tablespoons lime juice
1½ tablespoons fish sauce
1½ tablespoons honey
1–2 Thai chillies, sliced

For the salad
1 mango, peeled
1 red pepper, deseeded
1 carrot, peeled
2 spring onions, trimmed
A handful of coriander leaves,
 plus extra to serve
1 little gem lettuce, leaves
 separated

1. In a large bowl, mix together the ingredients for the marinade. Add the chicken breasts and leave to marinade for 30 minutes at room temperature.

2. Meanwhile, mix together the ingredients for the salad dressing and set aside. Preheat the grill.

3. Grill the chicken for 8–10 minutes, until just cooked through and beginning to brown. Cover with foil and allow to rest for 5 minutes.

4. Julienne the mango flesh and the vegetables and add to the bowl of dressing with the coriander. Stir to coat evenly.

4. Separate the little gem leaves and arrange three or four on each plate. Top with the dressed vegetables then slice the chicken and place on top. Garnish with more coriander leaves.

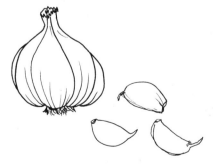

MAINS

PERSIAN LENTILS & HONEY VEG

*VEGETARIAN *DAIRY-FREE *GLUTEN-FREE

Delicious vegetables roasted with za'atar, a Middle Eastern spice blend (available from larger supermarkets) and served with herby lentils. Any combination of sweet root veggies will work here; add feta, too, if you like.

Serves 4

2 beetroots, scrubbed and quartered

1 large sweet potato, peeled and cut into chunks

2 medium carrots, peeled and cut into chunks

2 red onions, cut into eighths

2 tablespoons olive oil

2 teaspoons cumin seeds

2 teaspoons coriander seeds, crushed

1 tablespoon za'atar

2 x 250g pouches ready-prepared Puy lentils

A handful of dill, roughly chopped

A handful of mint leaves, roughly chopped

Seeds from 1 pomegranate

For the dressing

3 tablespoons olive oil

3 tablespoons pomegranate molasses

Juice of 2 clementines

3cm piece root ginger, peeled and grated

1½ tablespoons raw wild flower honey

1 garlic clove, grated

Squeeze of lemon juice

1. Preheat the oven to 180°C/gas mark 4. Spread the vegetables onto an oven tray, drizzle over the oil and sprinkle over the cumin and coriander. Season well and put into the oven to roast for about 20 minutes, until beginning to soften. Remove from the oven, sprinkle over the za'atar, stir gently and cook for another 20 minutes until caramelising around the edges.

2. Mix together the ingredients for the dressing, adding the lemon juice to taste.

3. Empty the Puy lentils into a pan and gently heat. Add the dressing and season well. Allow to cool slightly before stirring through half the herbs and pomegranate seeds.

4. Pile the lentils onto a platter, top with the vegetables and scatter with the remaining herbs and pomegranate seeds.

TOMATO & RUNNER BEAN BAKLAVA

*VEGETARIAN

This savoury baklava makes an excellent vegetarian main, served with a purslane or watercress, olive and caperberry salad with Ouzo-lemon vinaigrette, or is delicious served alongside roast lamb or grilled sardines. Served at room temperature, it even makes a great picnic food. For the best results, make the filling the day before to allow the flavours to infuse.

Serves 6-8

100ml olive oil
2 Spanish onions, halved and finely sliced
2 garlic cloves, finely chopped
2 teaspoons ground cinnamon
5 tablespoons tomato purée
10 vine-ripened plum tomatoes, skinned and roughly chopped
500g runner beans, stringed and cut into 4cm lengths
A pinch of sugar
1 bunch of dill (about 30g), finely chopped, or 2 tablespoons dried
1 packet of filo pastry (9 sheets)
100g melted butter
100g Greek or Medjool dates, stoned and finely sliced
250g feta, crumbled
6 tablespoons clear honey
Sea salt and freshly ground black pepper

1. Heat the olive oil in a large, heavy-based saucepan over a low heat and sauté the onions until softened and sticky; this can take up to 20 minutes. Add the garlic, cinnamon and tomato purée and cook for a further 2 minutes. Add the tomatoes and their juices and cook over a medium heat for about 8 minutes, before adding the runner beans, sugar, dill, a pinch of sea salt and 150ml water. Reduce the heat to a simmer and cook the beans for about 40 minutes, stirring occasionally, until the beans are soft and the sauce is nice and thick. Check the seasoning and cool before assembling.

2. Preheat the oven to 180°C/Gas 4. Unfold the pastry and cover with a damp cloth to prevent it from drying out. Brush a baking tray (about 30 x 20cm) with melted butter. Line the tin with a sheet of filo (cut to fit if too big), brush with butter and repeat until you have a three-layer thickness.

3. Spread half the tomato and bean mixture over the pastry, top with half each of the dates and feta. Sandwich another three layers of filo together with melted butter and place on top. Top with the remaining tomato mixture, dates and feta. Sandwich the remaining three filo sheets together as before and place on top.

4. Lightly score the top, cutting into diamonds about 10 x 5cm, or to desired size. Brush with the remaining butter and splash with a little water and cook for 35-45 minutes or until golden. Leave to cool slightly before serving, drizzling each portion with a little honey.

BEETROOT, GRAPE & WALNUT QUINOA

*VEGETARIAN *GLUTEN-FREE *DAIRY-FREE

A lovely salad which combines the rich toasty flavours of the quinoa and walnuts with sweetness from the grapes and a honey dressing.

Serves 4

200g red or mixed quinoa
50g walnut pieces
1 large beetroot, scrubbed
    and julienned
100g black grapes, halved
    and deseeded
100g watercress
Alfalfa or radish sprouts,
    to serve

For the dressing
3 tablespoons olive oil
1 tablespoon apple cider
    vinegar
2 teaspoons Dijon mustard
1½ teaspoons raw runny
    honey
Sea salt and freshly ground
    black pepper

1. Put the quinoa in a dry frying pan and toast over a medium heat for 3-4 minutes, stirring often. Add 400ml of water, cover the pan and cook for 10 minutes or so until the quinoa is soft and the grain cracks open. Leave to cool.

2. Mix together the ingredients for the dressing, seasoning to taste, and set aside.

3. Toast the walnuts in a dry frying pan over a low heat for 5 minutes, shaking regularly.

4. Tip the quinoa into a large bowl and add the walnuts, beetroot, grapes and watercress. Pour over the dressing and stir through. Season, then serve topped with some alfalfa or radish sprouts.

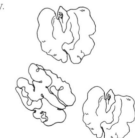

SALMON WITH MISO & HONEY GLAZE

*DAIRY-FREE

These sweet, salty flavours work fantastically with salmon. Some miso pastes are saltier than others so vary the amount of tamari you use accordingly.

Serves 4

200g brown rice
4 organic salmon steaks, skin on, or off as you prefer
200g Bok choy or broccoli
2 tablespoons sesame seeds, toasted
4 spring onions, finely sliced
Freshly ground black pepper

For the glaze
3 tablespoons sesame oil
3 tablespoons honey
4 tablespoons miso paste
1½ tablespoons tamari

1. Cook the rice according to the packet instructions. Preheat the grill and line a grill pan with foil.

2. In a bowl, mix together all the ingredients for the miso glaze, adding a good grinding of black pepper.

3. Place the salmon, skin side up, onto the grill pan and smear the glaze all over it.

4. Grill for 6–8 minutes, turning halfway, until just cooked through but still pink in the centre. Cook for a further 2 minutes if you like it well done. Cover and allow to rest.

5. Meanwhile, lightly steam the pak choi for 2 minutes.

6. Serve the salmon scattered with sesame seeds and spring onions, with the rice on the side.

TAMARIND PRAWNS
*DAIRY-FREE *GLUTEN-FREE

A yummy, spicy, tangy stir-fry. Buy the best prawns you can find, unpeeled, from either a fishmonger or Asian store if possible. They will be much sweeter and tastier than the regular supermarket peeled tiger prawns.

Serves 2–3

2 tablespoons coconut oil
600g raw king prawns, peeled and deveined
200g baby corn
200g sugar snap peas or mangetout
200g choi sum or pak choi, sliced
30g sesame seeds, toasted
Handful of coriander, roughly chopped
Rice or noodles, to serve

For the paste
4 small dried chillies
1 large banana shallot, chopped
15 dried shrimps (available from Asian stores and some supermarkets), soaked in 50ml boiling water
3 tablespoons tamarind paste
1½ tablespoons honey
3 large garlic cloves

1. In a high-speed blender or food-processor, blitz together the ingredients for the paste.

2. Heat half the oil in a pan and add the prawns. Cook on one side for a couple of minutes until brown, then add half the paste and cook for a further minute, until golden and cooked through. Remove to a plate.

3. Add the remaining oil to the pan and, when hot, add the vegetables. Stir -fry for 2 minutes, then add the remaining paste and 50ml of water. Cook for 2–3 minutes until coated in the paste and softened slightly but still crunchy. Add the prawns back to the pan and stir-fry everything together for another minute or two.

4. Stir through the coriander and sesame seeds, then serve with rice or noodles.

You could use chicken instead of prawns, if you'd prefer.

MEXICAN CHICKEN WITH SALSA *DAIRY-FREE *GLUTEN-FREE

Tasty chicken packed with smokey chilli flavours. You could use packets of ready rice for an easy, speedy meal.

Serves 3-4

1 tablespoon olive oil
1 onion, finely chopped
3 garlic cloves, finely chopped
1 teaspoon cumin seeds
150g basmati rice, rinsed
4 free-range or organic
   chicken breasts, skin on
1 corn on the cob, blanched
   for 4 minutes
1 x 400g tin black beans,
   drained and rinsed

For the marinade
Finely grated zest and juice
   of 1 lime
3 tablespoons chipotle paste
3 tablespoons Mexican honey
1 tablespoon olive oil
3 garlic cloves, grated

For the salsa
1 large ripe avocado
Juice of 1 lime
200g cherry tomatoes,
   chopped
4 spring onions, chopped
A handful of coriander,
   roughly chopped

1. Pre-soak 12 wooden skewers. In a medium saucepan with a lid, heat the oil and cook the onion gently until softened. Add the garlic and cumin and cook for a further minute.

2. Measure the rice and add to the pan with one and half times the volume of water. Bring to the boil, cover and cook for 10 minutes over a low heat, then turn off the heat and allow to steam for a further 10 minutes.

3. In a bowl, mix together the ingredients for the marinade. Place the chicken onto a board in between two large sheets of clingfilm. Bash the meat with a rolling pin to flatten it to an even thickness, about 1½ cm. Cut each breast into four strips. Add the chicken to the chipotle mix and allow to marinate for about 30 minutes (at room temperature).

4. Preheat the grill. Thread the chicken onto the skewers. Place onto a lined grill pan, along with the cooked corn cob, and grill for 6-8 minutes until the chicken is cooked through and the corn is slightly charred. Cover the chicken with foil and allow to rest for a couple of minutes.

5. Stand the corn on a board and slice off the kernels. Fluff up the rice with a fork and stir in the beans and corn.

6. For the salsa, cut the avocado in half, remove the stone, then remove the flesh using a tablespoon and roughly chop. Place in a bowl and squeeze over the lime juice, then stir in the remaining salsa ingredients.

7. Serve the rice topped with the chicken and a spoonful of salsa.

CHICKEN & APPLES
IN MUSTARD SAUCE
*DAIRY-FREE

Sweet honey paired with sharp apples makes a delicious combination, and this dish is perfect for an easy mid-week dinner. Serve it with either rice or pasta.

Serves 4

2 tablespoons seasoned dry
  breadcrumbs
4 x 115g chicken breasts
1 tablespoon olive oil
2 small unpeeled cooking
  apples (e.g. Bramley), cored
  and sliced
125ml chicken stock
A handful of freshly chopped
  chives, watercress or parsley

For the sauce
125ml apple cider
4 tablespoons honey (or more
  according to taste)
1 tablespoon mustard
1½ teaspoons cornflour
Salt and freshly ground black
  pepper

1. First make the sauce: whisk the cider, honey, mustard and cornflour with a pinch of salt and pepper to taste in a bowl. Put on one side.

2. Put the breadcrumbs in a bowl, add the chicken breasts and turn to lightly coat with crumbs.

3. In a large non-stick pan, heat the oil and add the chicken breasts. Cook over a medium heat until golden brown on one side, about 3-5 minutes. Turn the chicken, add the apples and cook until the chicken is browned on the other side.

4. Add the chicken stock, cover and simmer until the chicken is tender, about 15 minutes.

5. Carefully remove the chicken and apples to serving plates. Whisk the sauce again and add to the pan.

6. Cook over a high heat, stirring until lightly thickened and sizzling hot (this usually takes just 1-2 minutes). Spoon the sauce over the chicken and apples and sprinkle with chopped chives, watercress or parsley to serve.

HONEYED TURKEY & AVOCADO SALAD

Turkey is a great meat as it's full of amino acids and zinc and is also very lean. This salad makes a delicious, nutritious lunch and the avocado adds healthy fats, too.

Serves 2

8 asparagus spears
1 tablespoon runny honey
1 teaspoon soy sauce
300g turkey breast
100g watercress
200g cherry tomatoes, halved
1 avocado

For the dressing
2 tablespoons Greek-style
  yogurt
1 tablespoon chopped mint
Juice of 1 lemon
Salt and freshly ground black
  pepper

1. Preheat the grill to high. Place the asparagus on a baking tray and season well. Cook under the grill until tender, about 5 minutes. Leave the grill on for the turkey.

2. Mix the honey and soy sauce together and pour it over the turkey breast. Grill the turkey for 8 minutes on each side.

3. For the dressing, combine the yogurt, mint and lemon juice together and season well.

4. To serve, divide the asparagus, watercress, tomatoes and avocado between two plates, top with the sliced turkey and drizzle over the dressing.

BARBECUED DUCK
& FIGS *DAIRY-FREE *GLUTEN-FREE

A touch of sweetness is often just the thing for roasted duck. Honey scented with the enigmatic aroma of lavender makes a stunning combination, lifting the peppery roasted duck to a new level.

Serves 4

85g clover honey
1 tablespoon fresh lavender flowers
12 fresh figs, trimmed
1 tablespoon sunflower oil
4 duck breasts, trimmed and scored
Sea salt and freshly ground black pepper

For the sauce
480ml duck stock or chicken stock
480ml red wine (Barbera if possible)
1 tablespoon sunflower oil
1 large onion, diced
1 carrot, sliced
2 stalks of celery, diced
2 bay leaves
1 tablespoon peppercorns
4 sprigs fresh thyme

1. In a small bowl, combine the honey and lavender and leave for for 2 hours.

2. Meanwhile, make the sauce: in a medium saucepan over a high heat, bring the stock and wine to the boil. Simmer for about 1 hour, until reduced by half, skimming the top to remove any scum.

3. Start a charcoal or wood barbecue. When it has died down to coals, it is ready for use.

4. Heat the oil in a medium frying pan over a high heat, then add the onion, carrots, celery, bay leaves and peppercorns and cook until the onion browns, about 10 minutes.

5. Add the vegetables to the stock and wine mixture and simmer for 30 minutes, then strain the stock through a fine sieve, discarding the solids. Season with salt, add the thyme and keep warm.

6. In a small bowl, toss the figs in the oil. Grill the figs on the barbecue until lightly charred and warmed through.

7. Season the duck with salt on both sides. In a stainless-steel frying pan over a medium–low heat, gently cook the duck, skin side down, pouring the fat off occasionally, until the fat is fully rendered and the skin has become crisp, about 20 minutes.

8. Transfer the duck breasts to the barbecue and cook, skin side up, until the breasts begin to firm up and are pink inside, about 3-4 minutes. Transfer to a platter and lightly coat with the lavender honey. Leave to rest in a warm place for 5 minutes.

9. Slice the duck breasts into very thin slices. Divide the duck and the figs between four plates. Top the duck with the sauce and serve immediately.

FIVE-SPICE BEEF
WITH HONEY & SOY
*DAIRY-FREE

A rich and delicious marinade for beef. Use any mild tasting honey, and to make this a gluten-free meal simply choose a gluten-free brand of tamari.

Serves 4

2 x 200g sirloin steaks

2 teaspoons sesame oil, plus extra to drizzle

200g udon noodles

2 carrots, peeled and julienned

2 heads of pak choi or choi sum, shredded

3 spring onions, shredded

2 chillies, deseeded and thinly sliced (optional)

For the marinade

2½ tablespoons tamari, plus extra to drizzle

2 tablespoons Shaoxing vinegar

2 tablespoons orange flower honey

3cm piece of ginger, peeled and grated

1 fat garlic clove, grated

½ teaspoon Szechwan peppercorns, crushed (optional)

½ teaspoon five-spice powder

1. In a small bowl, combine the ingredients for the marinade. Put the steaks into a shallow bowl or plate, pour over the marinade and turn to coat the meat.

2. Heat half the sesame oil in a large pan. Add the steaks and cook without moving them for a minute and a half. (Check them after a minute as the honey might catch.) They should be nicely coloured but not charred. Turn and cook for 1 minute on the other side. Remove from the pan, cover and allow to rest for 5 minutes.

3. Cook the noodles according to the packet instructions, checking them just before

the time is up to ensure you don't overcook them. Drain thoroughly, tip into a large bowl and add the carrots, pak choi and spring onion. Mix well and season with a little sesame oil and tamari.

4. Serve the noodles in a pile, slice the steak thinly against the grain and pile on top. Sprinkle with some thinly sliced chilli, if you like.

MARINATED LAMB

This is spring on a plate! If you're using a boneless leg of lamb, add extra marinade and cook on a hot barbecue for about 8–10 minutes on either side, then rest well.

Serves 4

400g trimmed lamb neck fillet
  or boneless leg of lamb
A drizzle of olive oil
Pinch of dried oregano
4 tablespoons runny honey
Sea salt and freshly ground
  black pepper

For the feta curd
100g feta, crumbled
2 tablespoons lemon juice
5 tablespoons artichoke oil
  (from the jar, see tip)

For the peas
150g fresh peas (podded
  weight) or frozen petit pois
1 large garlic clove, crushed
20g mint leaves, chopped
20g dill, chopped
100g feta, crumbled
A little freshly grated lemon
  zest and 2 tablespoons juice
4 tablespoons olive or
  artichoke oil

To serve
1 small jar of artichokes
A handful of pea shoots
Extra-virgin olive oil

1. Rub the lamb with a little olive oil, salt, pepper and oregano. Leave to marinate for 30 minutes, or overnight in the fridge if you have time. Bring back to room temperature before cooking.

2. Preheat a griddle over a medium heat. Sear the meat for 4–5 minutes on each side (or cook to your liking), then remove from the griddle, drizzle with honey and rest in a warm place.

3. Meanwhile make the feta curd. Blend the feta, lemon juice and oil in a blender until smooth. Season with pepper and set aside.

4. In batches, lightly crush the peas in a pestle and mortar and transfer to a bowl. Stir in the crushed garlic, mint and dill, followed by the feta, lemon zest and juice and oil. Season.

5. To serve, smear the feta curd over your serving plates and spoon over some crushed peas. Quarter the jarred artichokes. Slice the lamb and divide evenly between the plates, then top with artichoke quarters and sprinkle with pea shoots. Drizzle with olive oil and serve.

This is a great way to use up the oil from a jar of artichokes but make sure you use artichokes marinated in olive rather than vegetable oil.

PLUM & LAVENDER BAKLAVA *VEGETARIAN

Not everyone would associate plums with Greek cuisine, but the succulent, tart plums cut through the sweetness of the baklava, while the lavender brings a touch of elegance with its delicate perfume.

Makes 20 pieces

11 red plums, halved, stoned
  and cut into thirds
100g lavender sugar, or
  100g caster sugar plus
  1 tablespoon dried lavender
300g roasted almonds, finely
  chopped
150g roasted hazelnuts, finely
  chopped
150g unsalted butter, melted
16 sheets (or 8 large sheets)
  of filo pastry
Greek-style yogurt or crème
  fraîche, to serve (optional)

For the syrup
250g lavender sugar or
  250g caster sugar plus
  2 tablespoons dried lavender
250g runny honey
2 strips of orange rind
1 cinnamon stick
250ml water

1. First make the syrup: put all the ingredients in a saucepan and bring to the boil, then simmer for about 5 minutes until it begins to thicken. Let cool, discarding the cinnamon stick and orange rind.

2. Preheat the oven to 200°C/ gas mark 6. Toss the plum slices with half of the lavender sugar in a roasting tin. Cover with foil and roast for 20 minutes, then remove the foil and cool. Strain off cooking juices and reserve.

3. Reduce the oven temperature to 180°C/gas mark 4. Mix the nuts with the remaining lavender sugar and set aside.

4. Brush the bottom of a 24 x 30cm baking tin with melted butter. If using large sheets of filo, cut in half lengthways. Brush one sheet with butter and top with another; repeat until you have a six layers. Sprinkle over a third of the nut mixture evenly, followed by a third of the plums.

5. Take another six layers of filo, brush each with butter as before, and lay on top of the nuts and plums. Scatter the pastry with more nuts and plums and repeat as above. To finish, brush the remaining four layers of filo with butter and place on the top. Using a sharp knife, score a diamond pattern on the surface, no deeper than the top layer of nuts. Brush with melted butter and sprinkle with a few drops of water to prevent the pastry from curling during cooking.

6. Bake for 35–40 minutes, or until golden. Remove from the oven and pour the cold syrup over the baklava and set aside to cool for a few hours, or overnight, until the syrup has been fully absorbed. Add the reserved plum juices to the syrup or reserve to fold through Greek yogurt. Serve at room temperature.

SEMIFREDDO WITH BRANDY BANANAS

*VEGETARIAN *GLUTEN-FREE

Semifreddo, or frozen parfait, is the closest you can get to ice cream without an ice-cream maker. The 'zabaglione' of eggs and honey stops the cream from crystallising and it sets beautifully. A chilled slice of this marries perfectly with hot brandy bananas.

Serves 4

For the semifreddo
90g runny honey
4 medium free-range egg
   yolks, beaten
150ml double cream
150g Greek-style yogurt
150g honeycomb, broken into
   small pieces

For the bananas
3 bananas
25g unsalted butter
2 tablespoons brandy

1. Line a 450g loaf tin with clingfilm.

2. For the semifreddo, warm the honey slightly in a small pan and slowly pour into the eggs, whisking at the same time, until the mix is light and fluffy.

3. Whip the cream in a large bowl until it forms soft peaks. Fold the yogurt into the cream and then carefully fold in the egg mixture. Finally, fold in the honeycomb and pour into the lined loaf tin. Place in the freezer overnight until frozen.

4. Just before you are ready to eat, slice the bananas. Heat up a frying pan. Add the butter, then the brandy and bananas and cook for 5 minutes.

5. Remove the semifreddo from the freezer and turn it out of the loaf tin. Peel off the clingfilm, then remove and slice the semifreddo and place on plates. Spoon the hot bananas over the semifreddo and serve.

HONEY, CINNAMON & YOGURT CHEESECAKE
*VEGETARIAN

This baked cheesecake is deliciously sweet and creamy, and lighter than it's traditional counterpart as it uses Greek yogurt as well as cream cheese. A touch of cinnamon compliments the sweetness of the honey and sultanas perfectly, adding an aromatic flourish.

Serves 12

300g digestive biscuits
100g unsalted butter, melted
Pinch of salt

For the filling
500g cream cheese
50g golden caster sugar
1 tablespoon cornflour
3 medium free-range eggs,
   beaten
200g Greek yogurt
Seeds from 1 vanilla pod
150g full-flavoured runny
   honey
1 teaspoon ground cinnamon
200g sultanas, soaked in
   boiling water and drained

For the topping
170g Greek yogurt
1 teaspoon vanilla extract

1. Preheat the oven to 160°C/ gas mark 3.

2. In a blender or large bowl, finely crush the digestive biscuits and mix thoroughly with the melted butter and a pinch of salt. Transfer the biscuit mix to a 30cm round springform cake tin and pack down carefully to cover the base. Place in the fridge to set for approximately 20 minutes.

3. In a large bowl, beat together the cream cheese, sugar and cornflour. Add the eggs, yogurt and vanilla seeds, then incorporate the honey, cinnamon and drained sultanas, stirring well to combine.

4. Tip the cream cheese mixture into the cake tin and spread to cover the biscuit base. Wrap the underside of the cake tin with

foil and place it in the middle of a large, deep roasting tray. Pour hot water into the tray until it reaches half way up the sides of the cake tin, then carefully place in the oven and cook for approximately 30 minutes.

5. For the topping, mix the yogurt and vanilla together in a small bowl with 50ml cold water. Remove the cheesecake from the oven and thinly spread the yogurt topping over the surface.

6. Increase the oven temperature to 180°C/gas mark 4. Return the cheesecake to the oven for a further 15 minutes. When the cake is just set, take it out and set aside to cool completely. Chill the cheesecake in the fridge overnight before slicing and serving.

PEACH ZABAGLIONE ICE CREAM *VEGETARIAN *GLUTEN-FREE

Although this is not strictly zabaglione, it does at least have all the necessary elements – plus a few extras. The honey gives it a slightly softer set. For best results, use ripe and juicy peaches: they will be easier to peel and will have a fabulous flavour.

Serves 6

4 large, ripe yellow-fleshed peaches
125g clear fragrant honey
Juice of ½ lemon
175ml full-fat milk
300ml double cream
½ vanilla pod, split in half lengthways
4 medium free-range egg yolks
75g caster sugar
2–3 tablespoons Marsala
A small pinch of salt

1. Cut a small cross on the underside of each peach. Place in a bowl, cover with boiling water and leave for 30 seconds. Drain and run cold water over to loosen the skins; they should now slip off easily with the aid of the knife. Cut the peaches into quarters, discarding the stones, and slice into wedges.

2. Bring the honey to the boil in a medium saucepan over a low–medium heat, then cook gently until reduced by nearly half and starting to darken to an amber-coloured caramel. Add the peaches and lemon juice, combine, and cook, stirring frequently for 8–10 minutes, until the peaches break down into a pulp. Using a stick blender or food-processor, blend the mixture until smooth.

3. Pour the milk and half the cream into a medium, heavy-bottomed pan. Add the split vanilla pod, bring slowly to the boil and then immediately remove from the heat and leave to infuse for 10 minutes.

4. Using an electric hand mixer, whisk the egg yolks with the sugar in a bowl until really pale and light. Add the Marsala and salt and whisk to combine. Reheat the milk, then pour onto the egg-yolk mixture and whisk constantly until smooth. Return to the pan and heat gently, stirring constantly, until thick enough to coat the back of a wooden spoon (don't allow it boil or you might scramble the eggs).

5. Remove from the heat, add the remaining cream and the peach purée and whisk to combine. Strain into a clean bowl and leave until completely cold. Cover and chill for at least 2 hours but preferably overnight.

6. Churn the mixture in an ice-cream maker according to the manufacturer's instructions, then scoop into a plastic freezer box and freeze until needed.

LAVENDER & HONEY TEA CAKE

*VEGETARIAN

Using yogurt in a cake mixture lends a certain depth of flavour and a moist crumb to a cake. Here, the tartness of the yogurt is set against the light floral notes of the lavender. This is an easy cake to make for a summer afternoon and is perfect with a cup of Earl Grey tea.

Serves 10–12

150g unsalted butter, softened
180g unrefined golden caster sugar
1 teaspoon vanilla extract
50g lavender honey (if you can't get it, use ordinary honey)
3 large free-range eggs
280g Greek-style yogurt
300g white spelt flour, sifted
2 teaspoons baking powder
½ teaspoon ground cinnamon

For the glaze

60ml lemon juice
6 teaspoons honey
250g unrefined icing sugar
2 teaspoons chopped dried, unsprayed lavender flowers

1. Preheat the oven to 160°C/ gas mark 3. Grease and flour a 24cm non-stick bundt tin.

2. In a large mixing bowl, beat the butter, sugar, vanilla and honey with an electric hand mixer until pale and fluffy. Add the eggs one at a time, beating well after each addition. Add the yogurt and stir until thoroughly combined. Fold through the flour, baking powder and cinnamon.

3. Scrape the mixture into the prepared bundt tin and bake in the oven for 35 minutes or until a skewer inserted into the middle comes out clean. Carefully remove the cake from the tin and place on a wire rack to cool completely.

4. While the cake is cooling, make the glaze. In a medium bowl, mix the lemon juice and honey, then whisk in enough icing sugar to make a thick, pourable glaze. Place the cake on a serving plate and spoon the glaze gently over the top, allowing it to run down the sides a little. Sprinkle over the chopped, dried lavender.

SPICED BANANA & COCONUT LOAF

*VEGETARIAN

If bananas go black, turn them into healthy banana cake. The loaves freeze well and are a great tea-time quick fix. Make this in a double batch, to use up a heap of banana in one go, and freeze either in slices or whole. If you like, you can add a handful of sultanas to the mixture, in which case, you'll also need to add an extra tablespoon of coconut milk.

Makes 10 thick slices

3 regular or 10 mini over-ripe bananas (about 300g flesh)
5–6 tablespoons light coconut milk
125ml coconut oil or light olive oil
100ml clear honey, ideally raw
2 medium free-range eggs
1½ teaspoons vanilla extract
75g plain flour, sifted
150g finely ground plain wholemeal flour, sifted
10g chia seeds
2 teaspoons baking powder
½ teaspoon five-spice powder
¾ teaspoon ground cinnamon
1 tablespoon shredded coconut (optional)

1. Preheat the oven to 170°C/gas mark 3. Grease and line a 900g loaf tin.

2. Mash the bananas thoroughly with a fork or stick blender.

3. Put the coconut milk (5 tablespoons if not adding shredded coconut, otherwise add 6), oil, honey, eggs and vanilla into a large bowl and whisk together until combined. Stir in the mashed banana.

4. In a separate bowl, lightly mix together the flours, chia seeds, baking powder, five-spice powder, cinnamon and coconut (if using), using a fork.

5. Sprinkle the dry ingredients over the oil and egg mixture and fold in using a large metal spoon until just combined. Turn into the prepared tin and bake on the middle shelf for 50–55 minutes or until rich brown in colour and a skewer inserted into the middle of the cake comes out clean.

6. Leave in the tin for 5 minutes, then turn onto a wire rack. Leave for at least 15 minutes, or until cool, before slicing.

If you are using finely ground wholemeal flour then sieve it; alternatively, just sprinkle it from a height to get as much air into the mixture as possible.

GINGER & HONEY TEA

*VEGETARIAN *DAIRY-FREE *GLUTEN-FREE

Raw honey is antimicrobial, anti-inflammatory, warming, soothing and great for digestion. Ginger is stimulating, warming and also good for digestion. Together they make an overall feel-good tea and a fantastic winter tonic. Add a slice of lemon to your cup if you wish.

Serves 4

1 tablespoon grated ginger
500ml boiling water
Local raw honey, to taste

1. Put the ginger and water in a small pan and boil for 5 minutes. Strain, allow the infusion to cool a little, then add the honey and serve.

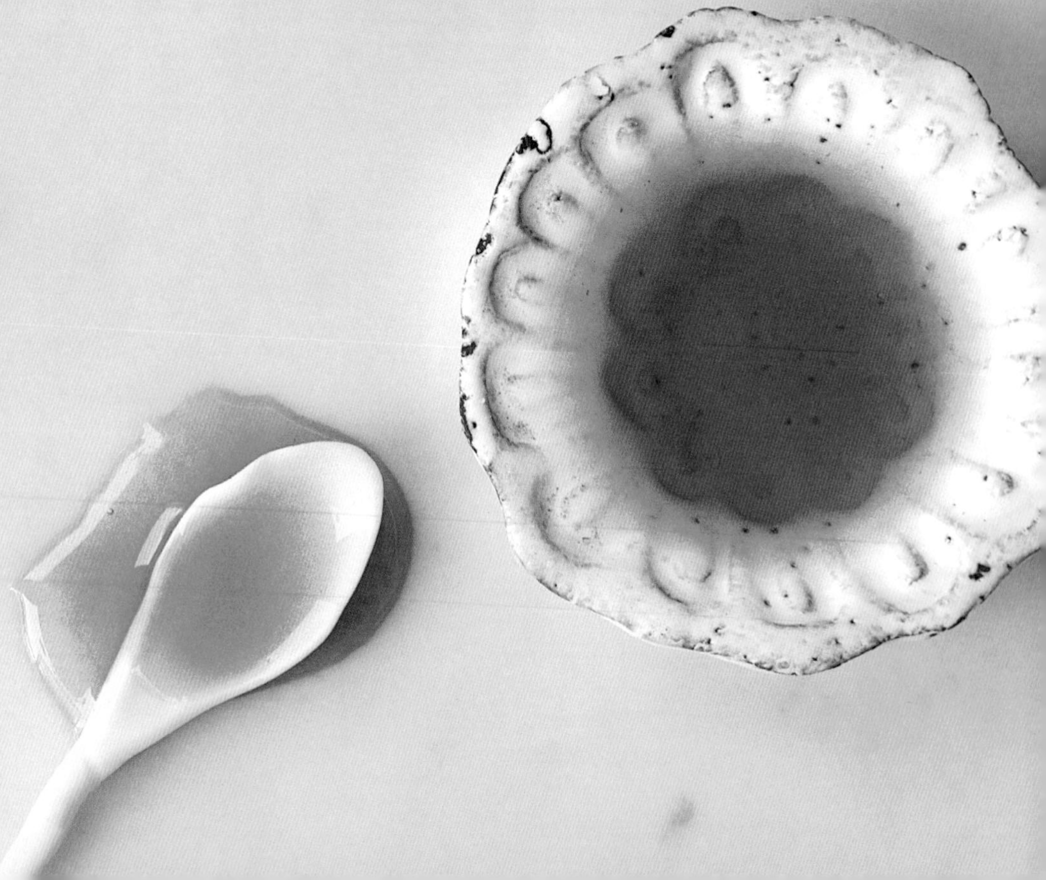

ORANGE, CINNAMON & HONEY CORDIAL

*VEGETARIAN *DAIRY-FREE *GLUTEN-FREE

An alternative to sugary lemonade. Dilute the cordial with still or sparkling water – or use it as a base for rum punch! Use more or less ginger depending on how spicy you like it.

Makes approx. 650ml

3 oranges
300g light brown sugar
2–4cm piece of ginger, peeled
  and finely grated
1 large cinnamon stick, split
5 tablespoons raw honey

1. Scrub the oranges lightly to clean them. Pare the zest of two of them, being careful not to take off too much of the bitter pith. (If you do, just scrape it off the rind with a knife.)

2. Put the zest into a saucepan with the sugar and 500ml of water. Bring to the boil, then stir well to dissolve the sugar. Add the ginger and cinnamon and turn off the heat. Leave to cool slightly then stir in the honey. Cover, refrigerate and allow to infuse for 24 hours.

3. Juice all three oranges and add to the cordial, then pour into sterilised jars. It will keep, refrigerated, for 2–3 weeks.

HONEYED CARROT
CUPCAKES *VEGETARIAN *DAIRY-FREE

This recipe uses no eggs or butter, which many people consider baking essentials. Instead, coconut milk does the job of binding the mixture and giving it moisture. You can easily double the quantities given here to make a dozen cupcakes.

Makes 6 cupcakes

150ml coconut milk
100ml honey
125g plain white stoneground
   flour
½ teaspoon bicarbonate of
   soda
¼ teaspoon baking powder
¼ teaspoon salt
½ teaspoon ground cinnamon
¼ teaspoon ground ginger
1 medium carrot, finely grated
2 tablespoons chopped
   walnuts
2 tablespoons raisins

1. Preheat the oven to 180°C/gas mark 4. Line a muffin tin with six cupcake liners.

2. Whisk together the coconut milk and honey. Sift in the flour, bicarbonate of soda, baking powder, salt and spices. Mix until smooth. Fold in the carrots, walnuts and raisins.

3. Divide the mix between the cupcake liners. Bake for 25–30 minutes, until a knife inserted through the centre of a cupcake comes out clean.

HONEY BISCUITS *VEGETARIAN

These simple biscuits are incredibly easy to make and sweetened only with delicious honey and dried fruit.

Makes 16–18

55g unsalted butter, chilled
115g plain flour
½ teaspoon bicarbonate of
  soda
55g sultanas
250ml runny honey

1. Preheat the oven to 180°C/ gas mark 4. Grease a square baking tin.

2. In a bowl, rub the butter into the flour. Dissolve the bicarbonate of soda in 1 tablespoon of hot water and stir into the butter and flour mixture, then scatter the sultanas into the mixture and stir in well.

3. Pour in the honey gradually and stir until you have a firm dough.

4. On a floured board, roll the dough out into a square shape approximately 1cm thick. Place in the prepared tin and score the top of the mixture into squares using a sharp knife.

5. Bake in the oven for 10–15 minutes. Leave to cool, then break into squares.

Eat these as a quick snack, or pair them with some fresh fruit and a scoop of ice cream or sorbet to enjoy as a dessert.

ANZAC BISCUITS

*VEGETARIAN

Anzac biscuits are so easy to make and are great as an after-school or teatime snack. They keep well and are a healthy alternative to shop-bought biscuits, which are often full of sugar.

Makes 20

125g white spelt flour
100g unsweetened desiccated
  coconut
50g dried blueberries
100g rolled oats
Pinch of salt
125g unsalted butter
85g dark honey
½ teaspoon bicarbonate of
  soda

1. Preheat the oven to 180°C/gas mark 4. Line two baking trays with greaseproof paper.

2. In a large bowl, stir together the flour, coconut, dried blueberries, oats and salt.

3. Melt the butter and honey in a small saucepan over a gentle heat, stirring until smooth.

4. Mix the bicarbonate of soda with 2 tablespoons of hot water, then add to the dry ingredients with the melted honey and butter and stir until combined.

5. Using your palms, roll pieces of the dough into balls about the size of a walnut and place on the prepared baking trays, allowing plenty of space between each ball. Flatten them slightly using the back of a fork and bake in the oven for about 15 minutes, or until golden brown.

6. Remove the biscuits from the oven and allow to cool on a wire rack before transferring them to an airtight jar or biscuit tin.

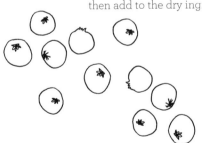

LEBKUCHEN *VEGETARIAN

This classic honey-sweetened gingerbread of Germany and Austria appears in many different forms there – from the shell of a gingerbread house to the biscuits that hang on the tree. The spices can be varied – a pinch of ground cardamom, cloves or nutmeg can be included, too – but ginger and cinnamon are essential. You can store the biscuits in an airtight container, un-iced or iced, for several weeks and they should improve in flavour.

Makes 18–20 stars

50g unsalted butter
100g golden caster sugar
100g runny honey
225g plain flour
½ teaspoon baking powder
½ teaspoon bicarbonate of
  soda
1 teaspoon ground ginger
1 teaspoon ground cinnamon
½ medium free-range egg
Vegetable oil, for greasing
Plain flour, for dusting

To decorate
White writing icing
String or ribbon, for hanging

1. Gently heat the butter, sugar and honey together in a small saucepan, stirring until smooth. Working off the heat, add the dry ingredients and stir until crumbly, then add the egg and work to a dough. If the mixture seems very sticky, you can add a little more flour.

2. Tip the dough out onto a worksurface, bring it into a ball and then pat it between your palms until smooth and shiny. Wrap in clingfilm, leave to cool and then chill for several hours or overnight.

3. Preheat the oven to 180°C/160°C fan/gas mark 4 and brush a couple of non-stick baking trays with vegetable oil.

4. Thinly roll out the dough on a lightly floured worksurface to a thickness of about 2mm and cut out 10cm stars. (If you don't

have a star-shaped biscuit cutter, you could make a template from thin card and cut around that.) Roll the dough twice only and arrange the biscuits on the baking trays – they don't spread much, so you can place them quite close together. If you want to hang them, make a hole at the base of one of the points of each star using a skewer.

5. Bake the biscuits for about 12 minutes until golden. (The lower tray may take a little longer.) The holes will have closed up slightly in the oven, so make them a bit larger using a skewer. Loosen the biscuits using a palette knife before they harden and become brittle, then transfer to a wire rack to cool.

6. Once the biscuits are cool, ice them as you fancy and leave this to set for an hour or two before storing or hanging the biscuits.

INDEX

A

antibacterial qualities 9–13
antifungal qualities 12
Anzac biscuits 89
apple: baked apple & cinnamon
 oatmeal 16
 chicken & apples in mustard sauce 62
avocado & honeyed turkey salad 63

B

baklava: plum & lavender 72
 tomato & runner bean 53
balsamic chilli vinaigrette 37
banana: semifreddo with brandy
 bananas 74
 spiced banana & coconut loaf 81
barrette croccanti 19
beans: tomato & runner bean
 baklava 53
beauty solutions 12
beef, five-spice beef with honey &
 soy 66
beetroot: beetroot, grape & walnut
 quinoa 54
 honey beetroot & feta 31
berries 16, 24–5, 89
berry & honey teff pancakes 23
bioflavonoids 10
biscuits: Anzac 89
 honey 87
 lebkuchen 90
blackberry & plum compote 25
brain function 12
brandy bananas & semifreddo 74

C

cakes: lavender & honey tea 78
 spiced banana & coconut loaf 81
 see also cupcakes
carrot: daikon & carrot salad 33
 honeyed carrot cupcakes 84
cheesecake, honey, cinnamon &
 yogurt 75
chicken: Balinese chicken 46
 chicken & apples in mustard sauce 62
 jasmine tea & honey chicken
 skewers 44
 Mexican chicken with salsa 60
chilli: chilli balsamic vinaigrette 37
 tomato, honey & chilli soup 40
cinnamon: baked apple & cinnamon
 oatmeal 16
 honey, cinnamon & yogurt
 cheesecake 75
 orange, cinnamon & honey cordial
 83
coconut: spiced banana & coconut
 loaf 81
cold and cough remedies 12
compotes: peach & raspberry 24
 plum & blackberry 25
cordial, orange, cinnamon & honey
 83
croutons 40
crystallised honey 9
cucumber salad 33
cupcakes, honeyed carrot 84

D

daikon & carrot salad 32
dressings 33, 36–7, 46, 51, 54, 57, 63
duck, barbecued duck & figs 64

E

energy bars, baked 26
energy drinks, instant 27

F

feta: feta curd 68
 fig-leaf wrapped feta 34
 honey beetroot & feta 31
fig: barbecued duck & figs 64
 fig-leaf wrapped feta 34
fructose 12

G

ginger: ginger & honey tea 82
 gingerbread 90
 sesame ginger lime 37
glaze, miso & honey 57
glucose 12
granola, fruity, nutty 20
grape, beetroot & walnut quinoa 54

H

heat-treated honey 9

I

ice cream, peach zabaglione 77
immune system boosters 12

J

jasmine tea & honey chicken skewers
 44

L

lamb, marinated 68
lavender: lavender & honey tea cake
  78
  lavender honey 10, 78
  plum & lavender baklava 72
laxative qualities 12
lebkuchen 90
lentil & honey Persian veg 51
lime: honey lime & soy king prawns
  43
  sesame ginger lime 37

M

marinades 46, 61, 66
marinated lamb 68
medicinal properties 12–13
miso & honey glaze 57
mustard: chicken & apples in
  mustard sauce 62
  honey mustard thyme 37

N

nutty, fruity granola 20

O

oat: baked apple & cinnamon
  oatmeal 16
orange, cinnamon & honey cordial 83
orange flower honey 10, 24–5, 66

P

pancakes, berry & honey teff
  23
peach: peach & raspberry compote 24
  peach zabaglione ice cream 77
plum: plum & blackberry
  compote 25
  plum & lavender baklava 72
prawn: honey lime & soy king prawns
  43
  tamarind prawns 59
preservative qualities 9, 13

Q

quinoa, beetroot, grape & walnut 54

R

raspberry & peach compote 24

S

salads: cucumber 33
  daikon & carrot 33
  honeyed turkey & avocado 63
salmon with miso & honey glaze 57
salsa with Mexican chicken 60
semifreddo with brandy bananas 74
sesame ginger lime dressing 37
soup, tomato, honey & chilli 40
soy: five-spice beef with honey &
  soy 66
  soy & honey lime king prawns 43
Spanish Blossom honey 39
storing honey 9
sugar 9, 12
super honey 11
sweetness of honey 9
syrup 72

T

tamarind prawns 59
tea: ginger & honey tea 82
  jasmine tea & honey chicken
  skewers 44
teff, berry & honey pancakes 23
thyme honey mustard dressing 37
tomato: tomato, honey & chilli
  soup 40
  tomato & runner bean baklava 52
turkey, honeyed turkey & avocado
  salad 63
types of honey 10–11

V

vegetables: foolproof root 39
  Persian lentil & honey 51
vinaigrette: chilli balsamic 37
  summer herb 37

W

walnut, beetroot & grape quinoa 54

Y

yogurt, honey & cinnamon
  cheesecake 75

Z

zabaglione peach ice cream 77

ACKNOWLEDGEMENTS

The publishers would like to thank the following for kind permission to reproduce their recipes:

James Duigan © p16 from *Clean & Lean For Life: The Cookbook*

Gino D'Acampo © p19 from *La Dolce Diet*; p31 from *Pronto!*

Gloria Havenhand © pp26, 27, 62, 87 from *Honey*

Ghillie James © pp33, 81 from *Asia Light*

Maria Elia © pp34, 53, 68, 72 from *Smashing Plates*

Rachel de Thample © pp37, 84 from *Less Meat More Veg*

Jimmy Garcia © pp39, 40 from *Social Eats*

James Tanner © p43 from *James Tanner Takes 5*

Helen & Lisa Tse © p44 from *Dim Sum*

Sophie Michell © pp63, 74, 75 from *Total Greek Yoghurt Cookbook*

Eric Skokan © p65 from *Farm, Fork, Food*

Annie Rigg © p77 from *Summer Berries & Autumn Fruits*

Amber Rose © pp78, 82, 89 from *Love Bake Nourish*

Annie Bell © p90 from *Annie Bell's Baking Bible*

First published in Great Britain in 2018
by Kyle Cathie Limited
Part of Octopus Publishing Group Limited
Carmelite House, 50 Victoria Embankment
London EC4Y 0DZ
www.kylebooks.co.uk

10 9 8 7 6 5 4 3

ISBN 978 0 85783 463 8

Text pages 20, 23, 24, 25, 46, 51, 54,
57, 59, 60, 66, 83 © 2018 Lizzie Harris
Design © 2018 Kyle Books
Illustrations © 2018 Jenni Desmond
Photographs © see below

Pages 2, 4, 5 (left and right), 13, 21, 22, 25,
    47, 50, 55, 56, 58, 61, 67, 95 © Faith Mason;
5 (middle), 27, 79, 82, 88 © Ali Allen;
6-7, 8, 11, 86 © Cristian Barnett;
17, 38, 41 © Clare Winfied;
18, 36, 85 © Peter Cassidy;
30 © Matt Russell;
32, 80 © Alicia Taylor;
35, 52, 69, 73 © Jenny Zarins;
42 © Anders Schonnemann;
45 © Gareth Morgans;
64, 91 © Con Poulos;
76 © Tara Fisher

Cover photographs: top row, left to right
© Faith Mason; Jenny Zarins; Faith Mason;
Faith Mason; second row, left to right
© Ali Allen; Gareth Morgans; Faith Mason;
Ali Allen.

Project Editor: Hannah Coughlin
Designer: Helen Bratby
Illustrator: Jenni Desmond
Production: Nic Jones and Gemma John

A Cataloguing in Publication record
for this title is available from the British
Library.

Colour reproduction by ALTA London
Printed and bound in China by C&C Offset
Printing Co., Ltd.